M000196203

Golden Moments

Words of Inspiration
By Sri Swami Satchidananda

Cover Art
By Peter Max

Library of Congress Cataloging in
Publication Data
Satchidananda, Swami.
Golden Moments

I. Title.
2012
IBSN 0-978-0-932040-90-9

Copyright © 2012
by Satchidananda Ashram–Yogaville, Inc.

All Rights Reserved. Except as permitted under
the U.S. Copyright Act of 1976, no part of this
publication may be reproduced, distributed or
transmitted in any form or by any means, or
stored in a database or retrieval system, without
the prior written permission of the publisher or
the copyright holder.

Printed in the United States of America.

Integral Yoga® Publications
Satchidananda Ashram–Yogaville
108 Yogaville Way, Buckingham, VA, USA 23921
www.YogaAndPeace.org

Books by
Sri Swami Satchidananda

Beyond Words

Enlightening Tales

The Golden Present

Bound To Be Free:
The Liberating Power
of Prison Yoga

The Healthy Vegetarian

Heaven on Earth

Integral Yoga Hatha

Kailash Journal

The Living Gita

To Know Your Self

Yoga Sutras of Patanjali

Titles in this special
Peter Max cover art series:

Meditation

The Key to Peace

Overcoming Obstacles

Adversity and Awakening

Satchidananda Sutras

Gems of Wisdom

Pathways to Peace

How to Find Happiness

The Be-Attitudes

Everything Will Come to You

Thou Art That:
How to Know Yourself

Free Yourself

The Guru Within

Books/Films about
Sri Swami Satchidananda

Sri Swami Satchidananda:
  Biography of a Yoga Master

Sri Swami Satchidananda:
  Portrait of a Modern Sage

The Master's Touch

Boundless Giving: The Life and Service of
  Sri Swami Satchidananda

Living Yoga: The life and teachings of
  Swami Satchidananda (DVD)

Many Paths, One Truth: The Interfaith
  Message of Swami Satchidananda (DVD)

The Essence of Yoga:
  The Path of Integral Yoga with
  Swami Satchidananda (DVD)

In the Footsteps of a Master:
  The 1970 World Peace Tour with Swami
  Satchidananda (DVD)

For a complete listing of books, CDs and DVDs:
  www.iydbooks.com

A Real Friend

A real friend should be able to help you in becoming a better person. Often we may find it difficult to travel alone. The path is steep. It's always better to have somebody who can help you, who can hold you and see that you don't slip. We should always look for such friends and, once we find them, we should never lose them.

A real friend will not hesitate to point out your mistakes. Those who hesitate are just there to exploit you. It's for their own benefit that they're keeping their friendship with you. They're afraid of losing it. A real friend will think of your benefit, not of his or her own. When will you know if a person is really a friend or not? Only when you are facing some difficulty.

Build Up Your Strength

You can build up your strength to the point where you are not influenced by your surroundings; in fact, you can influence the surroundings instead. You can change the environment if you have the strength of mind; but even if your mind isn't that strong, you can still have the strength not to be affected by the environment.

Learning not to be affected is an important step. If you are influenced by a situation, how can you change it? If fifteen people are crying and you go there and join them in the crying, you have simply added one more miserable person; you have not done anything to benefit people. Instead, if you are really strong and can maintain your own equanimity, all the fifteen people will be benefited by your strength.

We Are All Learning

Let's not deny anybody just because he or she follows a certain path or doesn't follow a certain path. Ultimately, we are all learning. If anyone is interested in knowing what practices you are doing, talk about it; explain how you have benefited, but don't try to persuade another to do the same thing.

That is what is meant by the *Biblical* saying, "Ask and it shall be given." You don't have to go and teach anyone. If someone asks, simply share what you know. If that person wants to do the same thing, fine. If not, if he or she wants to follow another path, that's fine too. With such an attitude you will learn to love everyone, respect everyone and there will be harmony in your life.

No Pain, No Gain

You should understand that no pain will come to you unless you do something to deserve it. If we deserve something, whether good or bad, it will come to us. If we don't deserve it, nobody can hurt us. No pain can come to us. Deserving means we have done something wrong and through that pain we have to purge it out.

Pain is a sort of purgation. Even if the whole world comes forward to give you pain, it cannot if you do not deserve it. But, unfortunately, we don't accept it that way. We simply say, "Oh, I am all innocent. This guy just came and hurt me." It's wrong thinking. Pain has no interest in coming to you unless you have invited it. Understand the purpose of the suffering, and accept it.

Always Choose Peace

When anything comes to you, first ask yourself, "Will I be maintaining my peace by getting this, or will my peace be disturbed?" Ask that for everything. People you would like to be with, possessions you would like to acquire. It doesn't matter what you want to do; strike that against the touchstone of peace. "Will this rob me of my peace?" If the answer is "Yes, you must choose peace or the other thing," you should always choose peace. If the answer is, "My peace will not be disturbed by it," okay, you can have that and still have your peace. That should be our aim.

A Worry-free Life

You might have the entire world at
your feet, but unless you have peace you
don't have a worriless life. What is the use
of having all these things around you? Care
more for your peace than for these. Without
that peace, nothing is going to make you
happy. If you have peace, even without
having anything else, you will be happy.

That's what you call contentment.
Whatever has to come will come. What will
not come, will not come. Why should I worry
about it? I know some of you might say,
"Then should I not do anything?" You should
do something, yes. Don't think that relaxation
or peace comes by not doing anything. No.
But when you are peaceful and content, you'll
be put to even greater use.

Experience Is the Best Teacher

The best teachers are your own mistakes. You learn even faster by your mistakes. Once I was at a conference with the great modern scientist Buckminster Fuller. He stood up and said, "Friends, forget about all the 'Do this. Don't do that' business. Commit as many mistakes as possible, as soon as possible. You'll become great!"

Every failure is a stepping stone. Remember, though, that you can't use the same stone for each step. Every step should be on a new stone. That means you shouldn't keep on making the same mistakes. Learn well from each one. The problem with many people is that they commit the same mistake over and over. Even so, they will eventually learn from that mistake and move on. Experience is the best teacher.

Correct Your Vision

We have to correct our vision. It's not only the eye that sees, but the "I" sees also. Sit in meditation and think, "Am I seeing things and people without any prejudice, or do I project my image?" We see not just the person, but our own prefixed notions. It's a very natural thing, and it's very hard to escape from that. When that happens, you have to question yourself. "Why am I seeing that person this way?"

A country proverb says, "Not every hole has a snake." You may happen to see a snake going into a hole; fine, remember that all holes are not free from snakes. But don't look for a snake in every hole you come across. See each one individually.

Thoughts are Powerful

Thoughts are more powerful than actions. Many great sages and saints who live in caves and remote areas just sit and pray for others. Those positive suggestions spread all over the globe. Thoughts are more powerful; there is no doubt about it. Many contemplative monks, nuns and other people sit and pray for the world.

Your physical strength, your material wealth, everything is given to you to be used for others. Of course that doesn't mean that you should not use it for yourself too; but the major part of it is to be offered to others. That's the way we should mold our lives. You should not think that you are living here for your own sake. We should be able to offer ourselves and our possessions for the benefit of humanity and the entire nature.

Real Love

Real love means you think of the welfare
of others. If others do something to you in
return, it's all right; accept it, but don't look
for it. "Only if you love me in return or if you
do this and this and that and that will I love
you. Otherwise I will not." All our problems
are caused by this.

We lose trust and become miserable when
love is conducted like a business. You will
not be happy with this kind of love. Don't
worry about the other person. Whether it is
between husband and wife or even between
two friends, if your relationship is based on
some gain from that person, you are never
going to be happy. The other person cannot
always give you what you want. So be
content just to love.

True Marriage

Marriage is equal sharing of life. You both go toward the goal together, helping each other. There should be assistance, not dependence. If you depend on the other person and you don't get what you were expecting, it will disturb your marriage.

True marriage means you don't expect anything from the other partner. You marry someone else to give all that you can. That's the end of it. You don't need to expect anything in return, not even love. The true purpose of a marriage is to give, not to ask for anything for yourself. Such a marriage is a spiritual marriage, one that is not bound by material dependency. You are together in spirit. That is what is meant by a marriage made in heaven. And it will last a long time.

Exercise Your Mastery

It is the nature of the mind to constantly change. You should learn how to surf on the waves of the mind, rather than being tossed and beaten by them. Always affirm that you are not going to be the slave of the mind; you are going to be the master. Exercise your mastery.

If something terrible comes, you think, "I can't stand it another minute." But if you just hold on a little longer, it passes. Sometimes white clouds come; sometimes black clouds come. Don't give up. When a restless cloud passes, you are peaceful again. If you give up and run somewhere else, there will be a difficult situation to face there too. Wherever you go, your own mind goes with you. If you can keep control over the mind, wherever you are will be a heaven.

Enjoy the Profit, Enjoy the Loss

To enjoy life to the fullest, stop wanting anything. If something comes, let it come. If it goes, let it go. Just be contented with what you have. Even if something goes from what you have, accept it. You should feel, "God gives me everything that I need, and God takes away everything that I don't need."

Then you will always enjoy what you have or what you lose. Enjoy the coming. Enjoy the going. Enjoy the profit. Enjoy the loss. The only way to enjoy is to just be what you are. If you are going to enjoy by getting things, you are going to be depressed by losing things. Nothing brings you joy. No person brings you joy. You yourself are joyful always. Depend on nothing, because nothing from outside can make you joyful.

Resistance Is Necessary

We are all searching for happiness and peace. Unfortunately, it doesn't come that easily. We have to go through many kinds of resistance. Why? Because only by passing through resistance do we become stronger. A seed needs some sort of resistance. That's why you dig a hole, put the seed in and cover it up. Then it says, "You think you are going to stop me here? I'm going to come up!" It pushes through and grows strong.

So don't look for the way of least resistance. Face the situation. Your own strength, your own mental courage will help you a lot. Once you feel that, "Yes, I can win it!" you will win. Be bold. Be strong. "I will achieve it." You need that will to achieve what you really want in life.

The World is a University

Nothing happens without a reason. The reason is to teach us some lesson. There is always a good lesson in whatever happens to us, even in the midst of our losses. I don't mean only in material losses; it's that way even with losses of our near and dear. The whole world is a university, and we are all here learning. Every individual should think, "I am the only student. Everyone and everything are my professors." All others are simply helping you to pass through.

In a way, even our kith and kin, our own near and dear are educating us to this truth. We should learn to understand and accept that.

The Path of Marriage

If you choose the path of marriage, it's a beautiful field in which to learn the great qualities of sharing and sacrificing. You are gradually dividing yourself, sharing your life with many others. You learn how to take care of them; you have more responsibility, and you are tested constantly. In school you are tested. Why? It helps you to find out whether you learned properly or not. It also helps others to know whether you studied well or not.

So in family life you also have tests to face. If you don't want to answer the questions and solve the problems there, if you just quit this examination and go somewhere else, eventually you will find an examiner standing in that place too. Wherever you go, you cannot escape from that.

Pleasure and Pain

Don't we respect both day and night?
We want both day and night. Night makes
the day complete. Pleasure and pain are
also two sides of the same coin. If you only
want pleasure and hate pain, you become
miserable. After one, the other is certain to
follow. When it comes and you don't want it,
you fight it. Instead, we must recognize that
life is like that.

If someone is nice to you and you
demand that he or she must always be nice to
you, always respect you, then you are seeing
only one side. If the other side comes, you
deny the person, you hate the person. You
should know that the other side will also be
there. Love that person for the other side
also. Respect them both.

Life is Filled With Tests

Life is filled with tests. But only lucky people will get tested. What is there to be learned from the experiences that test us? Without difficult experiences, you might have thought that you were a wonderful yogi because there was nothing to disturb you; everything seemed beautiful. Only when adversities come do you have an opportunity to prove what you have learned.

Losses are always great eye openers. This is the time to check to see how many things you are attached to. Are you suffering because you lost your possessions? Or are you undisturbed, happy and peaceful? Pleasures never open our eyes. It's only through pain that we learn our weaknesses.

Honest Business

It's competitive in the business world; and unfortunately or fortunately all the gimmicks seem to be paying off. A lot of money is made by gimmicks and false advertising. But if people come to realize that you are running an honest business, certainly they will come to you more. You'll never have difficulty in getting enough customers.

Business should be done with service in mind. Think of the benefit of the buyers. Your duty is to give them the right product or service at the right price with a marginal profit for you. You have to continue your business, so your profit can be a little above your overhead expenses to allow for rainy seasons. So you have every right to have a little profit; but not too much. Sell as if you were the buyer.

Tune Your Heart Radio

By sincere prayer you put yourself in a receptive mood. You become a good receiver. You tune your heart radio. Prayer is a form of tuning. Once you tune your heart through prayer, you get all the cosmic things. Whatever you pray for, you get. Pray for peace, you are tuning your radio to the peace station. Pray for beauty, you tune your radio to the beauty station.

A poet wrote: "More things are wrought by prayer than the world dreams of." We don't know the power of prayers. Don't we say, "You want it, you got it!" It is literally true; if you really want it sincerely, you get it.

Real want, sincere want, honest want is prayer. Through that sincere prayer, you tune your heart to God.

See Beauty

Judging others is an act of the ego; it's a kind of arrogance. Others may have a problem, but to judge them means that you have at least one kind of problem yourself, the problem of constantly criticizing people. You are actually no different from them.

An ordinary fly looks for filthy matter to sit on, while a honeybee will fly past many other things to look for even a little bit of nectar on a flower. You see certain things in others because you have the eye to see it. If you have a beautiful eye, you will see only beauty. A person who doesn't have any weakness at all won't even be on this earth. Don't have the kind of eye that finds faults in others. Be humble and correct your own problems.

Love Even the Mosquitoes

Universal love means to see the same Self
in everything. Unlimited, unconditional love
is universal. If you have universal love, there
is not even a single thing you dislike. You love
everything, even the mosquitoes that bite you.
You don't dislike them; you simply say, "Well,
mosquito, that is the purpose for which you
were created. You are doing your job in biting
me. I am doing my job and saying, 'Please get
out.'" You don't stop loving the mosquito. But
loving the mosquito doesn't mean allowing
it to bite you. Often people think, "Because I
love that mosquito, I cannot chase it away."
That's not so. You can love the poison, but
you don't have to swallow it.

Learn to Communicate

If you really want to help others, first know their nature. Will they really accept and appreciate your advice? If you are a little doubtful but you still want to say something, say, "You know, I had the same problem the other day, and I had two ways to act. Thank God I went this way. If I had done it the other way I would certainly have gotten into trouble. Luckily I chose this one. I'm just sharing this with you."

Put yourself in the other person's place. There is a gentle way of saying it. If you put things like this, he or she won't immediately feel defensive. Sometimes if you state the plain truth in plain language, you hurt the other person, and you get hurt as well. We have to learn how to communicate.

The Secret

Real joy comes when you work for others and not for yourself. When you work for yourself, you develop anxiety, you develop worry and fear. When you work for others there is joy. That is Karma Yoga, selfless service. Work for others or work in the name of God and the creation.

If the others need your service, it's their business to take care of you. You don't have to worry about taking care of yourself. Remember: If you decide to take care of yourself, you are the only person to take care of you. If you let others take care of you, so many will do that. That's the secret. Don't worry about taking care of yourself. Just think of others; then you will be taken care of.

Have A Strong Conviction

If you have conviction, it's easy to accomplish what you set out to do. But before you even begin, you must be convinced. Your thought should be, "This is what I want, no matter what happens. All the rest is nothing. I won't stop until I get it! This is the most important thing in my life."

Tests will come. Do you know how to install a flag post in the ground? You dig a hole, put the post in, put stones all around and hammer it to make it strong. Then you try to shake the post. As long as it keeps shaking, you keep on hammering. When do you stop hammering? When it stops shaking. Life is like that. As long as you are shaking, you'll be hammered.

Give Back

We receive constantly. Good thoughts, good food, good air, good rain. Even the smile from a baby is a gift. Whatever you get, you have to return it. You don't have to give it back at the same place. For example, if you get a fruit from the top of a tree, you can pour water at the root of the tree.

So do something to help someone–a poor person somewhere on the road, or a sick person. Somebody who needs a little help. That will balance it out. You got a smile from the baby, and you paid it back by helping that other person. You don't have to give it directly to the baby. We are constantly receiving. Every one of us should think, "How much am I receiving, and how much am I returning?"

Develop Your Will

We know what is wrong but we don't have the will power to stay away from that. How can one develop the will? By discipline and by regular practice. You develop that will by doing little, little, little things. Don't start with a big job that you cannot easily do; if you fail, you will lose confidence. Accomplishing small things will improve your self-confidence. Then one day, even the biggest thing will be the easiest thing for you.

Will means application of the mind. Training the mind. Making the mind work in a positive way. It's achieved slowly, slowly, slowly, slowly. It's easy to say, "Oh, I'm not made for that. It's too much for me. Not everyone can do that." Such excuses are self-delusion. Without will, we cannot achieve anything.

Do The Right Thing

Sometimes when you help somebody, you feel depressed. Why? It's because you had expectations: "I'm helping that person. The person should accept my help and get the benefit." When that person doesn't, you get upset. That means it's not a selfless act, it's a selfish act. "I did something and I want a result."

That doesn't mean there shouldn't be positive thoughts behind your actions. Certainly send your prayers, think about the welfare of the person. The difference is this: you want him or her to be happy of course, but you don't demand it. You're not attached to the outcome; you leave that to God.

In simple words, I would say an action without any selfish expectation whatsoever is a right action. Such an act will never disturb your mind or body.

The Golden Present

Don't waste your time in thinking about the past or worrying about the future. Some astrologers might be unhappy with me for saying that. They have a job to do; fine, let them do it. But don't get caught up in these things. You can rise above your planets. You are not your astrological sign. You are the pure Self. Your body and mind have limitations, it is true; but you can rise above them.

It really doesn't help much to know the future. It's the same for the past; it's better if you don't remember all the past lives. You might forget all your friends, but you will remember your enemies. Isn't it better to forget them? Let's not waste time on all these things. Think of the golden present. Enjoy the present.

It's All For Good

Our understanding is really very limited. For a long time I had this saying on my stationery: "It's all Your Name. It's all Your Form. It's all Your Deed. And it's all for good." Since childhood I believed that, and I have never regretted having that belief. It is that knowledge which keeps me peaceful; I never get upset over anything because it's all for good.

Maybe you will say, "Oh, that's an easy way of escaping," but all I get is peace. That is something more precious to me than everything in the world. You may call it escapism or blind faith. Whatever it is, I am retaining my peace. That's what I want. Because of that peace, I am always joyful and happy. I don't need to worry about anything.

Pass the Test

When you make a vow or a decision, don't expect it to go smoothly. If everything goes smoothly, where is the test to prove that you will stick to that vow? You should even be concerned if no tests come. If you vow not to eat sweets, soon someone will offer you the most tempting treat. If you vow to wake up every morning at 4:30 for meditation, suddenly you'll feel so tired.

If you vow to treat your spouse as God, probably at first he or she will look and act like a god. Then all of a sudden, that same god will turn into something terrible! Don't waver in your vow; continue to think of him or her as divine. If you pass the test, the situation has become a great instrument for your spiritual growth.

The Sign of a Healthy Person

What is the sign of a healthy person? You are relaxed everywhere–always at ease and in peace, within and without. Even in hell, you will be at ease. A healthy person hates no one, dislikes nothing. Total love, universal love emanates from within. There is no tension anywhere, no stress or friction. These are the signs of real health. A person who is healthy doesn't hurt anyone. Not only are you unafraid, but you see that others are not afraid of you. The "others" include animals, plants, everything. A healthy person emits always and only a loving and pure vibration.

Who will be the happiest person? The one who brings happiness to others. That means our minds should be well balanced under all conditions. That is Yoga.

Don't Worry About Tomorrow

Preparation for sleep is more important than sleeping itself. As soon as you walk into the house, don't just jump into bed and expect to get a good night's sleep. First, relax by releasing your soles/soul from your shoes. You can have a nice shower and put on some loose, comfortable clothing. As you loosen your body, loosen your mind also. Don't worry about tomorrow. Know that you have done today's job within your capacity.

With that, resign yourself completely and just relax. That will happen only when you put your trust in something higher. God sent you here and is working through you; God has done today's job. God may use you tomorrow. Be worriless like a baby. Don't put too much responsibility on your shoulders.

Be Good and Do Good

If you died this minute, what would people be saying about you? If the majority of people would feel sorry about your departure, if they would feel they had gotten a lot of help from you and that you hadn't hurt anyone, then certainly God is happy with you and the gates of heaven are open to you.

Let us think of these points and see if we can do something to make our life a little better, a little more peaceful, a little more useful. If it is not useful, at least let it be harmless. The essence of all religions is this: just be good and do good. Then God will be happy with you, and you will find real peace and joy in your life.

Clean Money

Don't work thinking only of your salary. Think of your job as an opportunity to serve, not just an opportunity to make money. If you work with that serviceful attitude, then whatever you make will be clean money, well-earned money that will certainly bring health and happiness to you.

It's not how much money we make, but how we make it that's important. If the money that you earned was not clean, it will be taken away by someone. If we can earn clean money we won't have these problems. Clean money comes from honest work. What you give should be at least a little more than what you get. That is what you call Karma Yoga. It will make the money that comes to you into clean money.

Understand the World

Don't expect the whole world to be enlightened one day. It would be like walking into a Detroit automobile factory and seeing only finished cars. If the factory were full of finished cars, it would no longer be a factory; it would become a showroom.

The universe itself is a university. People come as students; they study and learn. A few people get their diplomas and walk out. Don't think that one day the whole world will be enlightened. There will always be people who are still learning. When you understand the world, and realize your own true nature, you get the diploma. When others see you enjoying the peace and joy of having acquired that diploma, they will be inspired by you and will also work hard to get one. That is the world.

What You Gain,
You Should Not Lose

Never give up. What you gain, you should not lose. Whenever necessary, stop, build yourself up, regain your strength; and when the storm has cleared, continue to go forward. The mind has storms. It doesn't matter; just don't give up. Stay in the camp and wait for the storm to pass.

Make a resolution, "I will march forward a step at a time, no matter how slowly. I am never going to turn back. Even if I am not going to achieve anything in this life, it doesn't matter. I'll continue in the next life and the one after that, and the one after that. Never, never will I turn back." That kind of courage is necessary. It's a big task. The hardest thing in the world is to train one's own mind.

Unity in Diversity

We have had enough of fights and problems. If you realize this, you can begin right in your own home. Love your family, your pets, your plants. Do not treat them as something different from yourself. They all have the same essence, the same spirit. If we want to show the unity in diversity, that is where we can begin. You may be angry with your husband or wife, but do not put the pot down with a bang. Be gentle. See the same spirit in everything. That is unity in diversity.

There is nothing without life in this world. Be gentle, be nice, be loving. See your own Self in all and treat everything properly. That is how to show the unity in diversity visibly and powerfully. A real spiritual experience means to see the unity in diversity.

Karma

Whatever method of healing you use, don't expect someone else to do all the work for you. When people send prayer requests to us, we ask them to pray also. It isn't: "You go ahead and do whatever you want. I'll pray for you and you'll get well." That's not right. That's interfering with someone's karma. The people who are affected should practice certain disciplines.

There is nothing wrong in looking for some remedy for a problem. If your karma is really strong, even with all the remedies, the ailment won't get cured. If that happens, you should know it's because of some karma and accept it. If somebody comes to help you, then your karma is bringing somebody to help. You should accept that too.

You Don't Have to Be Allergic to Anything

Many people complain about allergies. They are always saying, "I am allergic to this, allergic to that." Allergy is not something coming from outside; allergy comes from lack of health. If your body is strong enough, you don't have to be allergic to anything. Keep the body in good shape. That means giving it the proper exercise and eating the right food in the right quantity.

If you keep the body healthy, the body can adjust to anything. Above all, have the proper thoughts. If you constantly complain of disease, you will have disease. As you think so you become. If you think, "I am weak, I am weak, I am weak," you are certainly going to be weak. Never allow the mind to worry about anything.

It Is Better to Learn Soon

Selfishness can never make you happy. Sometimes you may get what you want, but your own selfishness will spoil it. In a way, that is what we learn from all these disappointments in life. Every time you approach something with a selfish motive, it literally hits you on the head. Unfortunately, many people don't learn from a single hit or even a hundred hits. On the other hand, sensible people will learn the lesson just by seeing others getting hit.

Don't ever think that you will escape. You are going to learn the lesson. Until you learn the lesson this will happen again and again and again. So it is better to learn soon–the sooner, the better–so that you can enjoy the rest of your life with all joy and peace.

Realize Your Own True Nature

Know that you are already liberated. The true Self is eternally pure, unchanging, immortal, never tainted by anything. It is always peaceful. But you don't see your true Self; you see the image of your true Self on the mirror of the mind. So when the mind gets tossed, the image is disturbed. The image seems to be assuming qualities because of the mind. So you look at the image and say, "See, I'm bound." But in truth, you are never bound.

If you still feel that you have to liberate yourself, the only liberation to be achieved is to liberate the mind from the selfishness that creates all these disturbances in the mind. Liberate yourself from the personal ego and you will be always peaceful; you will realize the true nature of your own Self.

Remember the Truth

Don't give room for temporary depressions. Things come and go. Nothing is permanent in this world. Even our bodies come and go. You once had a young body; now you have an adult body. Someday you will have an old body. It's the body that goes through all these changes.

You are immortal. Identify with the real "I." Remember that truth always. Apply this whenever you are in a depressed state. Shake it off and say, "I am a lion! This is all just temporary. I have come across this before and I know it will go away." You can heal yourself. There's a beautiful part of the mind, a powerful part of the mind, that can always get you out of any problem. Use that part, and don't succumb to the other side of the mind.

Live Like a Lotus in the Water

A lotus flower grows in very shallow water, usually in a muddy area. Though it comes out of the mud and mire, it rises as a beautiful flower that lives in the water without being affected by it. The lotus flower is always given as an example for one who wants to live spiritually in the world. The lotus leaf is right in the water, but it's never moistened by the water. When you pick it up, it's completely dry. It never gets wet. If you throw a little water over it, the water will roll off and scatter around like pearls.

A person should live like the lotus, being in the world but not affected by it. You should always express your natural beauty, though you may grow in a dirty place. Nothing from outside should affect you.

You Are Free

Ultimately, we are all looking for happiness. But it's not something that has to be brought in from outside. Happiness is already within us, and is to be experienced. If we want to experience that joy within, we have to liberate ourselves from our own self-made bondage.

Nobody on earth is interested in binding you. Even if someone were interested, nobody could do that. It's completely in your hands to be bound or to be free. If you think that you are bound, you are bound. If you think that you are free right this moment, then you are free. So, the freedom or the joy of freedom has to come from right thinking—from not thinking that you are bound. Who is a free person? The one who is interested in liberating himself or herself from self-made bondage.

You Are Part of the Cosmic Mind

All the thoughts that the entire world is thinking and will think and has thought before are already in the cosmic mind. They are there waiting for you to draw upon. Actually, there is nothing new; nothing can be created and nothing can be destroyed. Nobody has ever "created" any new thinking.

We are receiving constantly. And we receive according to our tuning. The music is there, but if you tune to the wrong station you will get atmospheric disturbance. Both are there. You call it "disturbance" because you don't want it, but it is there. The music also is there. So we simply tune to receive. Your mind is nothing but a part of the cosmic mind, and a part of the cosmic mind is functioning through you.

Be Married to Your Peace and Joy

Relationships need not be difficult. If you don't have any selfish purpose, then you don't expect anything and you don't lose anything. You are just there together. When you are apart, you are apart. You aren't attached to that relationship.

Realize that you don't have to have a relationship to be happy. You are already married to your peace and joy. But you don't appreciate that. That means you don't realize your own true nature, which is happiness. The minute you realize that you are always happy, that you are always peaceful whether you have a relationship or not, that you have a permanent relationship within, then you no longer worry about an outside relationship. If it comes, fine, if it doesn't come, wonderful. You become independent. You don't depend on anything or anyone for your happiness.

Think Well, You Will Be Well

"As you think, so you become." Think well, you will be well. Think ill, you will be ill. It's all your thought. Sometimes you might not be thinking ill of yourself, but you are thinking ill of others. That is still thinking ill. Whether it is about you or somebody else, that is what you are thinking. When you think of that, you will become that.

That is why we say, "See no evil, hear no evil, speak no evil." If you see evil, hear evil, speak evil, you will become evil. It's not to save others that you are asked not to think ill, not to speak ill. You will not be hurting them, but you will be hurting yourself. In our lives we should always think well. Train your eyes to see the bright side of everything.

Selfless Selfishness

Selfishness is when you feel, "I must have it at any cost." Analyze your motives. "What am I gaining out of that?" By being selfish, you aren't going to be happy at all. Any time you are unhappy, if you look for the cause, you will see that you were selfish in your approach or in your thinking. That's why a selfish person can never, never, never be happy.

Even wanting to be peaceful at all times is selfish. But that kind of selfishness isn't wrong. If you find the peace in you, people all around you will be benefited by your peaceful nature. Even if you don't consciously do anything for them or say anything to them, you'll be setting an example, and they'll learn from your example. So that's a sort of selfless selfishness.

Enjoy Everything You Do

It's not the action that is important,
but how you do it. To decide whether you
are doing something in the right way ask
yourself, "Am I maintaining my peace while
doing this?" If the answer is "No," then you
are doing something wrong. Everything you
do should make you happy, jubilant. You
should enjoy it, whatever it is, and feel like
doing more. You should forget yourself while
you are doing it.

Work should be fun, not a burden. If you
become heavy while doing it, then you are
doing it as a labor. Even if you look for a
thank you, you are looking for some reward.
When you do something for a reward, it's
labor. It's not service. Labor means you do
it to get it. Service means you just do it, and
forget it.

Never Forget What You Receive

Think about the great benefits and gifts you have been constantly receiving. The more you think of them, the more you feel grateful, the more you feel devoted, the more you feel love. But unfortunately, our tendency is to forget all the nice gifts, and instead to remember the one small thing that we did not get.

Never forget what you received that is good, even though it is small; but don't even remember it for a minute if somebody has done some harm to you. Even this one teaching is enough to help us to see friends, and friends and only friends, everywhere.

If You Want It, You've Got It

Commitment is very important in life. Those who want to lead a spiritual life are here to change things and to build a better world. Let nothing shake you. You have to be really bold and strong to achieve anything in life. Be that bold. When you know that something is right, don't hesitate to follow it.

Certainly there may be obstacles, tests; but don't give up. Even if you should fall down or make a mistake, get up and say, "No! The next time I'll be strong." Keep on going, like great mountain climbers, until you reach the top. If you really want to do it, you will be given the needed strength. You will have all the support. If you want it, you've got it; but your want has to be that strong.

Accept It and Seek Help

Illness can be karmic; the reaction to your past actions. The best way to deal with that is to know that it is your past karma that has brought this. Pray sincerely, "God, let me accept this and do whatever I can to clean it up." It doesn't mean that you shouldn't seek help from others. Accept the illness and seek help. The mere acceptance will take away half the pain of the illness.

The illness becomes painful when you deny it, when you don't want it. So, accepting the karmic reaction is an important thing. But sometimes people don't have the proper understanding and they say, "Oh, it's my karma. What can I do about it?" That is wrong. You do what you can.

The Value of Peace

Anything that becomes rare becomes very dear to us. It's only when a species is labeled "endangered" that we try to protect it. Even the value of peace has been taught to us in this way.

Peace is also a species on the verge of extinction. The whole world is now striving to save it. Let us do whatever we can to help others and to not consciously hurt anyone or anything.

That means that no one should be afraid of you and you do not have to be afraid of anyone. This is an important quality of a yogi or spiritual seeker. Fearlessness is an important virtue. Develop that.

Don't Worry About the Future

What you sow you reap. Don't worry about the future and don't worry about the past. A great thinker said the past and the future are not even visible. But what is visible? The golden present. Sow good thoughts, sow good deeds, and I am sure you will reap good fruits. Do the right thing in the present, and don't worry about the future. The people who worry about the future miss the present as well.

Always remember the golden present. Never miss it. A happier life is not given to you by someone else. Not even God can give you a happier life. Remember that. Happiness is in you. If you take care not to lose it, it is always there.

My Simple Prayer

Would you like to know my prayer? My prayer is very simple. "God, I know that it is all Your form. It's all Your name. It's all Your deed. And it's all for good."

You are an instrument in the hands of the Super Consciousness; it functions through you as an individual consciousness. You are a little cell, and that Cosmic Consciousness makes you function. You don't do anything, so why worry about anything? All you have to do is know, "Yes, God is working through me. Credit or demerit goes to God. I am not responsible. I am simply an instrument." If your life is like that, if you fully realize this truth, where is the difficulty for you? You can be totally, totally free from any problem in life. I'm positive about that.

Burdens Are Simply Rocks in the Mind

If you enjoy living, you enjoy working; the joy itself is enough to put a lot of strength in you. If you don't enjoy living and working, life becomes a burden to you and weakens you. People who don't enjoy their activities get tired very soon. If you really enjoy what you are doing, you will never get tired. Feeling tired is mainly in the mind. When you don't like something, it becomes very heavy to you. You carry it as a burden.

Suppose you are asked to carry a big rock. You might say, "Oh, it's too much, I can't carry it." But suppose I give you a big bundle of gold coins even heavier than that rock? Somehow you will find the strength to drag it. That shows that burdens are simply rocks in the mind.

People Are Like Mirrors

When others criticize you, there are two things to think of. First, "That's the way they look at me and that's what they see." Give them that freedom. Probably they may not see the other, better side. Leave it at that.

The other thing to think about is, "Yes, that person is like a mirror. Through him or her I see my defects." You go in front of a mirror to clean the dirty spots from your face. In the same way, this person is revealing your dirty spots. Thank the person and work on it. Then you will even look for criticism, because you can get help from that. If people don't criticize you, you will never know your own defects. If you see it in this light, you will never be angered by that.

Self-Healing

By putting out positive thoughts, and correcting your mistakes, you can heal your problems. But don't do something to alleviate the problem without correcting the cause. The suffering came for your benefit. You should not try to take that away. Instead, bring out the nice things, the good qualities in you, the positive side in you and the negative will get cured by itself.

Self-healing should be that way. If you have some problem, ask yourself, "How did I get into this? What is the cause?" Then make a resolution: "Yes, in the future I will not encourage such thoughts. I will cultivate the opposite." The best way to drive away the darkness is to bring light into the room.

Think In a Positive Way

Sometimes we get frightened and a fear gets into the subconscious mind. Consciously din into the mind that you are immortal and that there is nothing to be afraid of. Think in a positive way. Convince your conscious mind, and let the conviction sink into the subconscious mind.

You can even make a tape of your own, put it under your pillow and literally sleep on it. It will slowly sink into your subconscious mind. The fear has gone into the subconscious, and you need to replace it with positive thoughts. Put reminders everywhere until it's completely rooted out. The yogic way is to put a new, opposite thought into the mind so that the undesirable thought will be squeezed out. And if you can't do it all by yourself, get help from others.

You Are The Pure Self

Unless we realize our own true nature, unless we become aware of our spiritual reality, our life's purpose is not fulfilled. The main goal behind all these searches and approaches and actions is to realize our true nature, to realize the Self, the God within, and thus to realize that everything is the expression of that same Spirit.

It doesn't matter what you do, your goal should be to come close to this understanding: "Essentially I am God's spirit, I am the pure Self, I am Existence-Knowledge-Bliss Absolute." Ascertain your true nature, your spiritual nature. You are only functioning through this body and mind. They are your vehicles. You are not the body. You are not the mind. But you are that immortal soul.

Healing Energies

We should know that the breath and the mind are intertwined. Wherever one goes, the other follows. When the mind becomes agitated, the breath becomes agitated. When the mind is totally peaceful, the breath almost comes to a stop. So in the same way you can direct the breath with your thoughts. You can send the *prana* or vital energy wherever you want.

The same principle applies to healing also. By sending your thoughts to any affected part, you send your *prana*. Self-healing is possible. In a way, even when you pray for healing that's what you are doing. You trust that the higher power, God, is helping you to heal that. And you believe it. So you are communicating with the higher power, and that energy automatically goes to the affected part along with your little energy.

What Came for Your Head Took Away Your Hat

Selfish thoughts disturb the mind. When the mind is disturbed, the body gets disturbed. That is why the condition of the mind is very important. If the mind is serene and peaceful, many accidents could be avoided.

By keeping your mind calm, you can win over your karma. If you have peace of mind, even if karma comes you may not know it. It will just come. There is a South Indian saying, "What came for your head, took away your hat." The karma came to take your head, but because of your peace of mind and presence of mind, it just took your hat away. That was enough to nullify the karma.

Even if the karma is really going to affect you, let it affect you. But remain peaceful. Stay calm, cool and live in the golden present.

The Body-Mind Connection

The mind's physical expression is what you call the body. Change the mind, and you can change the body. That's why your face changes when your mind is happy. It glows. People don't see your mind, but they see your face. When your mind is unhappy, don't they say, "Hey, what's wrong?" Why? Because the face expresses the mind. Every cell will listen to the mind and get changed according to its moods.

That's why when you are in a very depressed state, you can't even get up or do anything. You say, "Oh, I can't do a thing today. I'm so upset." Getting upset is in the mind. But the body and mind are interconnected. If one falls sick, the other will also fall sick. That is why we have to take care of both.

Mistakes are Part of Learning

Perfection doesn't come overnight. Making mistakes is part of learning so, when you make a mistake, don't get upset. Learn from your mistakes, and then don't repeat them. You are free to make another kind of mistake, but not the same mistake. Every mistake, every failure is a stepping stone for future success.

You have to fail. Look at Olympic champions, great runners. Did they run out of the womb at birth? Did they start life running? No. They couldn't even move their bodies much. How long did it take for those future champions to be able to stand? To walk? To run? How many times did they fall? That is the process of learning. Don't be afraid of falling. Let every failure help you to learn a little better for your future success.

Accept Things As They Are

The minute you learn to respect and see both sides of the coin as equally good, you can enjoy both. You never hate anything. It's only a matter of your understanding and acceptance. Then you enjoy everything in life. Everything! There's nothing, nothing, nothing that is terrible, bad or negative in this life.

Let us have that light of understanding. Accept things as they are, people as they are. Don't demand anything. Don't put conditions: "Only when you do this does it prove that you love me." Rise above all this. Our attitude, our approach, our love should be unconditional. Simply accept people for what they are, as they are. Learn to love everyone and everyone will love you, no doubt. Then, life is worth living. The world becomes a heaven on earth for you.

Do Your Work With Joy

In nature, every job is equally important. There is no superior or inferior work. You can perform any work with joy if you know that every job is equally good. You lose the joy of doing things when you don't understand the importance of them, when you compare your work with someone else's work.

There is no blue collar work, white collar work. If you want to see it that way, your legs are doing blue collar work. Your head is doing white collar work. Your blue collar workers have to take the white collar worker wherever it wants to go. We are the ones who create all this superiority/inferiority. The world needs everything. Every action is equally good. Do them all with joy.

The Buddy Within

You cannot give beyond your capacity. In the name of helping others, you should not put your body into a situation where it might get hurt. You don't have to feel guilty about it. Your conscience will tell you if you are just finding an excuse. Nobody expects you to go beyond your capacity.

Ask advice from your own pure Self. The conscience is constantly giving us advice, but often we don't listen to it. You should learn to ask that buddy within. Sometimes you might feel a conflict: "I don't know which is the Self and which is the ego." Ultimately, we have to develop the capacity to discriminate within ourselves. That is why meditation is so important. Until you become established in that, at least in meditation you should be able to hear your own inner Self.

You Are Unique

We should always roar like lions, "I am that I am! I am ever joyful, ever peaceful! We must have that strength and courage. Even if you act temporarily, "I am a super yogi!" for one week, you will see the difference. Don't say, "Oh, that's only fit for saints. I'm just an ordinary person." You are not ordinary.

If you were ordinary, you wouldn't even be here. Nobody is ordinary here. No. Even a thorn has a purpose. It has been placed here for a particular cause and it's unique in its place. Nothing can be substituted for that. Nobody can replace you. You are unique in your position. Don't try to compare yourself with others. You are all-important. Everybody is needed in this cosmos. Be proud of your existence.

Adapt and Adjust

It is easy to sit and meditate. The most difficult part is to practice bearing insult and injury, learning to adapt, adjust and accommodate. These are the teachings of the great sage of the Himalayas, Sri Swami Sivananda. You can do your spiritual practices all by yourself. But what about your attitude when you deal with people day in and day out? That's where you have to prove that you have achieved something in your spiritual practices.

If you practice adapting, adjusting and accommodating, you will never point a finger at others and blame them. Even if another person is at fault, if you know how to adapt, adjust and accommodate, you are able to rise above those situations. That needs a tremendous capacity to keep the mind totally under your thumb.

Better to Be Humble

Realize that nothing is yours. You didn't come with anything and you are not going to go with anything. Things were given to you along the way. At a certain period things and people came to you. At a certain period, they might go again.

So what is this "mine, mine, mine" business? Many "mines" bring many explosions. Don't identify yourself with your possessions. How many ex-millionaires are paupers now? How many great men who once ruled countries are now begging? What is permanent? Think about all these things. All the beauty queens, where are they now? What is there to be egotistical about?

Don't be attached to things. If they come, let them come. Remembering these things will take our pride away. It's always better to be humble, with our feet on the ground, so we don't fall.

Only Love Will Heal Hatred

It takes more courage and strength to smile at a person who hates you than to hit back. It's here that the idea of karma can be helpful. If somebody just comes and hits you for no reason, stop and think to yourself, "Probably this is my karma. I must have hit somebody sometime in the past and escaped from getting hit or being punished for it. Now this person is returning what I gave out." Accept it.

Certainly there's no effect without a cause. Nobody can come and hurt you if you are really that innocent. You should thank that person: "You have helped me to purge this karma at last. Thank you so much." At the same time you are teaching the person a lesson. Only love, not more hatred, will heal hatred.

Become a Friend

You don't make a friend. You become a friend. Then you automatically will have friends. If you relate to people by loving and caring, sharing and helping, then naturally they will see you as a good friend. When they see you as a good friend, then they become your friends. It begins with you. Never hurt anyone's feelings.

The secret is to always look for opportunities to help others; look for ways to be nice to them. Sometimes they might even be nasty to you; if so, ignore it, forget it. Maybe that's the way they are; but don't retaliate with the same kind of words. The great sage Thiruvalluvar said that if people do something wrong to you or hurt you, do something really good for them in return. That's the best punishment.

Failures Are Stepping Stones

Failures are stepping stones to future success. If you're going to brood over your past mistakes and be afraid that something terrible will happen, you'll just waste your time. Nature's grace is such that it will pardon any mistake, because only by mistakes do you learn. If a child is going to think of all the falls it had while it was learning to walk, it will never walk. So treat the falls as stepping stones.

If you have the opportunity to see the people you wronged, go to them with all courage and apologize. Say, "I made a mistake. I didn't know what I was doing. Please excuse me." That's the only way to repay your debts. If you cannot see these people, if they are not here anymore, at least mentally pray for them.

By Giving You Never Lose

Give until it hurts, but don't lose your peace. It's all right not to help others if it will help you in preserving your own peace. If you're going to lose your peace, then how are you going to help others? When you're easeful and peaceful, then you can be useful. Otherwise, you may even harm rather than help the situation.

Don't do something if you know that by doing it you're going to disturb your peace. Maintaining your peace is more important. But at the same time, give as much as you can. Even if you get hurt, it doesn't matter. Give. Because by giving, you never lose. There is a joy in thinking of others first. You will have more peace and joy in doing that.

Giving Advice

If you want to give some advice, your first duty is to look and see if that person will accept it, if he or she will be benefited by your saying something. If the person gets upset, it shows that you don't know how to say it gently in the proper way.

Stop and think, "Is this the right moment to discuss this?" If you positively know that the person is not in a mood to receive it from you, wait until another time or start very gently. Maybe at the spur of the moment the ego will come and say, "How dare you tell me that!" But when you go away, he or she will try to apply your advice. Remember there is a giver and a receiver; both have lessons to learn.

Don't Worry

Don't worry about anything. Worry never brings any benefit to anyone. On the other hand, it spoils even the little that you might do. There's a beautiful saying I read on a daily calendar page. It said, "Sorrow is nothing but what you borrow." Nobody is going to give you that. You go and borrow it. You are the cause of your worry. Nobody can bring worry to you.

Worry will sap away even the little energy, the little capacity, that we may have. A worried doctor cannot operate, you all know that. A worried student cannot write an exam. Go with full confidence. Just say, "I'm doing all that I can." Everything takes its own time. We are in a hurry to change things. We want everything instantaneously. Let it go smoothly in its own time.

Think of the Good
Qualities in Others

If you are jealous, it affects you physically and mentally. It in no way helps you or anyone else. So at least for your own sake, it's advisable not to have that. Every time you feel that kind of emotion, immediately think, "Is it not affecting me? And who is the cause of it? Myself! So at least for my own sake, I should stop it."

Jealousy means that when others are doing well, you feel unhappy about it. Maybe they're not running after things; they're contented with what they have. They put themselves in the position to receive. By thinking of the good qualities of others, you will also develop them and your life will be so beautiful. Automatically when you feel that contentment, things will come to you by themselves. People will like you, appreciate you too.

Obstacles Draw Out Capabilities

Life is always a challenge. Many times you will feel like giving up. Facing the challenge is difficult, giving up is easy. But where is the guarantee that you won't face the same challenge somewhere else or even a *bigger* challenge?

When you are facing a difficult situation, there are two approaches you can take. One is, "Let me stay put and face the challenge, try to understand it, learn the lesson and rise above it." The other approach is to just walk out. But remember: The same kind of challenge will come again, in a little different form. Why? Because difficulties come to make us strong. Life is an obstacle race, and a challenge has been presented to you to draw out your inner capabilities. Nothing is impossible to achieve.

The Essence is the Same

Love everyone and everything equally. By loving everything, you are really loving yourself. Everything is nothing but the expression of yourself. If you stand in front of a mirror, you love that reflection. You smile at it and it smiles at you. In the same way, the whole world is your projection. You love because you are made of love; not because you have to love.

The scriptures say to love your neighbor as your Self. You don't love your neighbor as an individual; you love that person as your Self. That means you have to see your Self in the other person. Real love is possible only when you see everything as your own expression. When we go beyond the name and form, we will find that the essence is the same.

About Sri Swami Satchidananda

Sri Swami Satchidananda was one of the first Yoga masters to bring the classical Yoga tradition to the West. He taught Yoga postures to Americans, introduced them to meditation, vegetarian diet and a more compassionate lifestyle.

During this period of cultural awakening, iconic pop artist Peter Max and a small circle of his artist friends beseeched the Swami to extend his brief stop in New York City so they could learn from him the secret of finding physical, mental and spiritual health, peace and enlightenment.

Three years later, he led some half a million American youth in chanting *OM*, when he delivered the official opening remarks at the 1969 Woodstock Music and Art Festival and he became known as "the Woodstock Guru."

The distinctive teachings he brought with him blend the physical discipline of Yoga, the spiritual philosophy of *Vedantic* literature and the interfaith ideals he pioneered.

These techniques and concepts influenced a generation and spawned a Yoga culture that is flourishing today. Today, over twenty million Americans practice Yoga as a means for managing stress, promoting health, slowing down the aging process and creating a more meaningful life.

The teachings of Swami Satchidananda have spread into the mainstream and thousands of people now teach Yoga. Integral Yoga® is the foundation for Dr. Dean Ornish's landmark work in reversing heart disease and Dr. Michael Lerner's noted Commonweal Cancer Help program.

Today, Integral Yoga Institutes, teaching centers and certified teachers throughout the United States and abroad offer classes and training programs in all aspects of Integral Yoga.

In 1979, Sri Swamiji was inspired to establish Satchidananda Ashram–Yogaville. Based on his teachings, it is a place where people of different faiths and backgrounds can come to realize their essential oneness.

One of the focal points of Yogaville is the Light Of Truth Universal Shrine (LOTUS). This unique interfaith shrine honors the Spirit that unites all the world religions, while celebrating their diversity. People from all over the world come there to meditate and pray.

Over the years, Sri Swamiji received many honors for his public service, including the Juliet Hollister Interfaith Award presented at the United Nations and in 2002 the U Thant Peace Award.

In addition, he served on the advisory boards of many Yoga, world peace and interfaith organizations. He is the author of many books on Yoga and is the subject of the documentary, *Living Yoga: The life and teachings of Swami Satchidananda.*

In 2002, he entered *Mahasamadhi* (a God-realized soul's conscious final exit from the body).

For more information, visit: www.swamisatchidananda.org

About Peter Max

Peter Max, one of America's most famous living artists, is also a pop culture icon. His bold colors, uplifting images and uncommon artistic diversity have touched almost every phase of American culture and have inspired many generations.

In 1966, Peter Max met Swami Satchidananda in Paris, invited him to America and helped him to found the Integral Yoga® Institute. Inspired by his friendship with Swami Satchidananda and the Yoga teachings he learned from him, Max created his signature style of cosmic scenes and characters, painted in bold, vibrant colors. It was among the most influential graphic sources of the 1960s and was often cited by journalists and art critics as the visual counterpart to the music of The Beatles.

Cited as "America's Painter Laureate," Peter Max has painted portraits of six U.S.

Presidents and his impressionistic paintings of the Statue of Liberty and American flag art are on display in Presidential Libraries and U.S. Embassies.

Max's work in portraiture has extended to world leaders (Mikhail Gorbachev, Nelson Mandela, H. H. The Dalai Lama, Dr. Martin Luther King, Jr.), CEOs (Richard Branson, Sumner Redstone) and major figures in the world of sports and entertainment.

His exhibitions have had record-smashing attendance at such venues as the de Young Museum, the Hermitage Museum and the Moscow Academy of Art. And, although he has produced major work in traditional media, such as canvas, paper, bronze and ceramic, he has also demonstrated how fine art can enrich non-traditional media, such as a U.S. postage stamp, a Continental Airlines' super jet and a 600-foot stage set for the 1999 Woodstock Music Festival.

As official artist for more major cultural events than any other contemporary artist, Max has championed the causes of peace, ecology, democracy, human and animal rights and charity–confirming that he is not only one of America's most prolific living artists, but also one of the most relevant.

For more information, please visit: petermax.com